FIRST COOK BOOK

Written by Harriet Hains
Illustrated by Claire Boyce

‖ •PARRAGON• ‖

A PARRAGON BOOK

Published by Parragon Book Service Ltd,
Units 13-17, Avonbridge Trading Estate, Atlantic Road,
Avonmouth, Bristol BS11 9QD

Produced by The Templar Company plc,
Pippbrook Mill, London Road, Dorking, Surrey RH4 1JE

Copyright © 1995 Parragon Book Service Limited

Edited by Robert Snedden
Designed by Mark Summersby

All rights reserved.

Printed and bound in Great Britain

ISBN 0 75251 210 2

Contents

Kitchen Safety

If you are sensible and careful you will be quite safe in the kitchen. However, there are dangers and you should remember the following rules:

Ask an adult to be with you if you are using the oven or heating fat or water on the hob.

•

Always wear oven gloves when you take things out of the oven.

•

Cut with the knife blade facing away from you.

•

Turn saucepan handles inwards towards the back of the cooker.

•

Don't turn the heat up too high when boiling water or cooking fat.

•

Never touch electric sockets with wet hands.

Throughout this book measurements are given in two ways to help you. Whenever the measurement says tablespoon or teaspoon it means level spoons, not heaped ones.

To measure liquid use a jug with measurements on the side. Read it at eye level.

Useful measurements

600ml (1 pint) = 20 fluid ounces
2 tablespoons = 30ml (1fl oz)
3 teaspoons = 1 tablespoon
25g (1 oz) flour = 3 level tablespoons
25g (1 oz) caster sugar = 2 level tablespoons
25g (1 oz) lard or butter = 2 level tablespoons

Cowboy Baked Beans

You will need:

a chopping board • a knife • a tin opener • a saucepan •
a tablespoon • a teaspoon • a wooden spoon • bowls to serve

---

1 small onion • 2 tablespoons vegetable oil
two 439g (15½ oz) tins baked beans
3 teaspoons ready-made mustard
25g (1oz) soft, brown sugar • 1 tablespoon vinegar
225g (8oz) frankfurter sausages • salt and pepper

Serves 4

1. Peel the onion and chop it up finely on the chopping board. Heat the oil in the saucepan. When it's hot, carefully add the onion, and fry for 5 minutes until soft. Turn off the heat.

2. Open the tins of baked beans and pour into the saucepan. Add the mustard, sugar and vinegar and stir into the baked beans with the wooden spoon. Keep stirring until the sugar has dissolved.

3. Slice the frankfurters into 2cm (3/4in) pieces on the chopping board. Put these into the bean mixture, then heat for about 5 minutes until hot, stirring all the time.

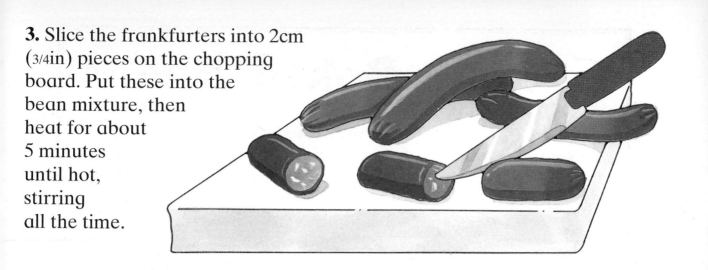

4. Add a pinch of salt and a little pepper. Serve in heated bowls.

You can warm the bowls by filling them with hot water while you are cooking.

Stuffed Potatoes

You will need:
a baking tray • a fork • a spoon • a chopping board • a knife
a mixing bowl • a cheese grater • a potato masher

4 large, scrubbed potatoes • 60g (2oz) butter
90g (3oz) chopped ham
(or small tin of baked beans for vegetarians)
90g (3oz) cheese • a little milk • vegetable oil
1 tablespoon chopped parsley
1 tablespoon chopped chives (if available) • salt and pepper

Oven setting: 200°C/400°F - Gas mark 6

Serves 4

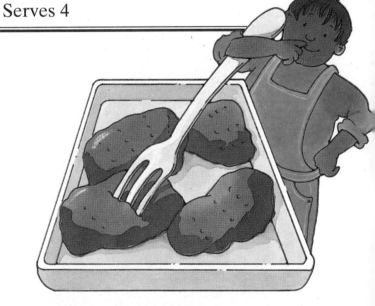

1. Preheat the oven. Prick the potatoes all over with the fork, rub them with vegetable oil and sprinkle with salt. Put them on the baking tray. Bake in the oven for 1 hour.

2. Using oven gloves, lift the baking tray out of the oven, and stick a fork in the biggest potato to see if it is done. If it is soft it is cooked.

3. Leave the cooked potatoes to cool for 10 minutes. Then carefully cut them in half lengthways. Spoon the soft, white potato into a bowl.

4. Carefully grate the cheese into a bowl. Mind your fingers! Mash the potato in the bowl, then add all the other ingredients, stirring well together. Fill the potato skins with the mixture.

Put the stuffed potato skins back in the oven and bake for another 15 minutes. Serve with salad or vegetables of your choice.

Sweet and Sour Chicken

You will need:

a shallow oven-proof baking dish • tin foil • a tablespoon
a small jug • oven gloves

---

4 skinned chicken breasts • juice of 1 small lemon
juice of 2 large oranges • 1½ tablespoons soy sauce • butter
clear honey • salt and pepper

Oven setting: 150°C/300°F - Gas mark 2

Serves 4

1. Preheat the oven and then use the butter to grease all round the baking dish.

2. Spread a spoonful of clear honey across the top of each chicken breast and put them side by side in the baking dish.

3. Mix together the orange juice, lemon juice and soy sauce in a small jug. Then add a pinch of salt and a little pepper and pour the mixture over the chicken.

4. Cover the baking dish with tin foil and bake in the oven for about 40 minutes. Then, using oven gloves, lift out the baking dish to see if the chicken is cooked

You can see if the chicken is cooked by poking it with a fork. If the juices are pink it needs more time in the oven.

5. Serve the chicken with the sauce poured over it. Eat it with rice and salad, or try it with Courgette Bake (page 16).

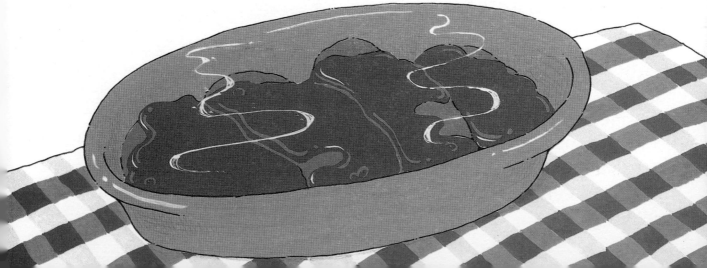

Vegetarian Courgette Bake

You will need:

a shallow baking dish • a saucepan • a colander • a hand whisk
a small mixing bowl • a sharp knife • a chopping board
a cheese grater

1kg (2lb) courgettes • 3 eggs • 275ml (1/2 pint) single cream
125g (4oz) cheese • salt and pepper • butter

Oven setting: 200°C/400°F - Gas mark 6

Serves 4

1. Preheat the oven and grease the baking dish with the butter.

2. Wash and slice the courgettes and cook them in a saucepan of boiling, salted water for 3 to 4 minutes.

3. Put the colander in the sink and very carefully pour the courgettes into the colander to drain away the water.

Watch out! Boiling water is dangerous. Ask an adult to do this.

4. Whisk the eggs and cream together in the mixing bowl and season with salt and pepper. Now carefully grate the cheese into a bowl. (Keep your knuckles away from the grater!)

5. Put the courgettes into the baking dish and cover with the creamy egg mixture. Sprinkle the grated cheese on top.

6. Bake the courgettes for about 20 minutes until the cheese turns golden brown.

Serve with baked potatoes or hot French bread.

Perfect Pizzas

You will need:
a mixing bowl • a sieve • a teaspoon • a tablespoon
a wooden spoon • a large, flat baking tray • a tin opener
oven gloves

250g (8oz) plain flour • 1 teaspoon salt
2 teaspoons of 'easy blend' dried yeast
1 400g (14 oz) tin tomatoes • 1 tablespoon tomato puree
1 teaspoon oregano (dried or fresh) • 125g (4oz) grated cheese
125g (4oz) mushrooms

Oven setting: 230°C/450°F - Gas mark 8

Serves 4

To Make The Dough

Home-made bread dough takes a long time to rise, so start making it two hours before you want to eat the pizzas.

1. Sieve the flour and salt into a bowl. Mix in the 'easy blend' yeast, then add just enough warm water to make a soft ball of dough that does not stick to the bowl.

This is called kneading

2. Put your dough on to a work surface sprinkled with flour. Fold the dough over, press it down with your knuckles and turn it. Do this for about 5 minutes until the dough is stretchy and smooth.

18

3. Now put the dough in a greased bowl, cover it with a clean tea towel, and put it in a warm place for about an hour.

4. When the dough has doubled in size, take it out of the bowl and knead it for another 5 minutes. Split it into four balls and put them on a greased baking tray.

5. Press the balls of dough and flatten them out. Raise the edges slightly. Preheat the oven.

To Make The Tomato Sauce

1. Pour the tin of tomatoes through the sieve into a mixing bowl. Use the wooden spoon to rub the tomatoes through the holes. Throw away the skins.

2. Add the tomato puree, salt and pepper, and stir. Spread the sauce on to each pizza base and sprinkle with cheese, oregano and sliced mushrooms or any other of your favourite toppings.

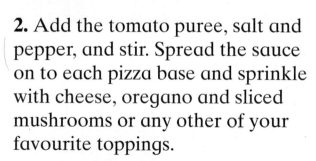

3. Now put the pizzas on the middle shelf of the oven and bake for 20-30 minutes until crisp round the edges.

Crispy Bacon and Avocado Salad

You will need:

a large salad bowl • salad servers • a chopping board
a sharp knife • kitchen roll • a grill pan • a colander
an empty jar with a screw-top lid • a jug

---

a large, crisp lettuce • 8 rashers of lean bacon
1 large, ripe avocado • half a cucumber • 1 eating apple
1 tablespoon chopped parsley • 1 teaspoon brown sugar
1/2 teaspoon mustard powder • salt and pepper • 4 tablespoons oil
1 tablespoon vinegar • 1 tablespoon lemon juice

Serves 4

To Make the French Dressing

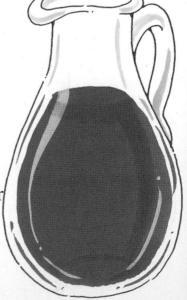

1. Put the vinegar, oil, lemon juice, mustard and brown sugar into the jar. Season with the salt and pepper.

2. Screw the lid of the jar on tightly and shake the contents well for about a minute. Pour into a jug ready to serve.

To Make the Salad

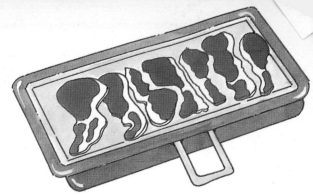

1. Wash and dry the lettuce. Throw away any tough leaves. Shred the lettuce and put it into the bowl.

2. Chop up the cucumber and apple. Peel the avocado and cut the flesh into medium-sized chunks. Mix with the lettuce.

3. Cut the rind off the bacon rashers and grill under a low to medium heat for about 6 minutes or until crisp, turning occasionally.

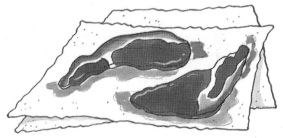

4. Spread some kitchen roll on the work surface and put the bacon on this to absorb the fat.

5. Slice the warm bacon into small pieces. Gently mix the pieces into the salad. Sprinkle with parsley.

Serve while the bacon is still warm with the jug of French dressing

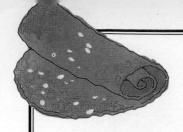
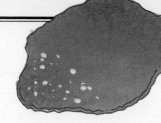

Pancakes

You will need:

a large mixing bowl • a sieve • a large jug •a wooden spoon
a small frying pan • a palette knife • an oven-proof dish • tin foil
a sharp knife • a chopping board

---

2 eggs • 125g (4oz) plain flour • pinch of salt
300ml (1/2pint) milk • 5g (1/4oz) butter • caster sugar • jam
2 lemons chopped into eights • lemon juice

Serves eight

1. Sift the flour and salt into the mixing bowl. Make a hollow in the centre down to the bottom of the bowl, and break the eggs into it.

2. Add half the milk and very gradually mix in the flour from the sides, beating with a wooden spoon.

3. Do this until the batter is smooth and then stir in the rest of the milk. Leave the mixture to stand for one hour, then pour into the jug.

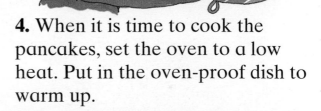

4. When it is time to cook the pancakes, set the oven to a low heat. Put in the oven-proof dish to warm up.

5. Melt the butter in the frying pan and swirl it round. When it is hot, pour in some batter from the jug. Tilt the pan very carefully in all directions so that a thin layer of batter covers the base of the pan.

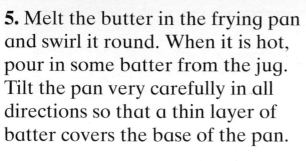

Take care! hot fat is dangerous.

6. Cook the pancake until bubbles appear in the mixture and the edges turn brown. Use the palette knife to flip the pancake over and cook it on the other side.

7. Put the pancake into the warmed oven-proof dish, sprinkle with lemon juice and caster sugar and roll it up. Cover with tin foil and put back in the oven to keep warm.

8. Make more pancakes in the same way until all the batter is used up. Heat some plates at the bottom of the oven. Serve each pancake on a warm plate with a wedge of lemon. You can also serve them with honey or jam.

Chocolate Pudding

This pudding should be made the day before you want to eat it.

You will need:

2 mixing bowls • a wooden spoon • a hand whisk
a shallow serving dish • a palette knife

125g (4oz) fresh, white breadcrumbs
(Ask an adult to make these for you.)
125g (4oz) drinking chocolate • 50g (2oz) demerara sugar
1 teaspoon instant coffee • 600ml (1 pint) whipping cream
a banana or an orange

Serves up to six

1. Put the grated breadcrumbs, drinking chocolate, sugar and coffee in a bowl and mix together with a wooden spoon.

2. In the other bowl, whisk the whipping cream with the hand whisk until it is thick and stands up in peaks. (This will take about 10 minutes, so keep going!)

3. Spread a layer of cream across the bottom of the serving dish with the palette knife. Then sprinkle a layer of the dry mixture over the top.

4. Gently spread another layer of cream across the top of that, and then add another layer of the dry mixture. Carry on building up layers until all the ingredients have been used up.

5. Leave the pudding overnight in a cool place (but not a fridge or freezer). Before serving, decorate the pudding with slices of fresh orange or banana.

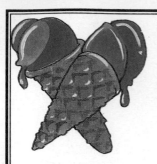

Raspberry Ice Cream

Ask an adult to watch over you for this recipe as boiling sugar is dangerous.

You will need:

a sieve • 2 mixing bowls • a wooden spoon • a hand whisk
a saucepan • a plastic freezer container

450g (1lb) fresh raspberries • 175g (6oz) caster sugar
150ml (5 fl oz) water • 275ml (1/2 pint) thick double cream

Serves up to ten

1. Put the raspberries into the sieve and use the wooden spoon to rub them through into the mixing bowl below. Throw away any pips that are left behind.

2. Put the sugar and water into the saucepan. Stir over a medium heat until the sugar has dissolved. Let it come to the boil, and boil for 3 minutes until it becomes a syrup.

3. Remove the syrup from the heat and stir into the fruit.

4. Whip the cream with the hand whisk. When it is thick, very slowly stir the cream into the fruit and syrup until it is evenly mixed.

Take the ice cream out of the freezer and put it in the main part of the fridge 1 hour before eating.

5. Pour the mixture into the plastic container and put the lid on. Put into the freezer or the ice-making compartment of the fridge (on its coldest setting) for 3 to 4 hours. Eat within 3 weeks.

Cheese Dip

You will need:
a serving bowl • a wooden spoon
a mixing bowl

---

4 tablespoons cream cheese
2 tablespoons sour cream
1 teaspoon chopped chives
a squeeze of lemon juice
salt and pepper

Mix all the ingredients together in the mixing bowl, season with salt and pepper and spoon into the serving bowl.

Boil the eggs in the saucepan for about 10 minutes. Carefully empty away the boiling water, and cover the eggs with cold water. When cool, peel and chop the eggs and mix with the mayonnaise until smooth. Scoop into a serving dish.

Egg Mayonnaise Dip

You will need:
a serving dish • a knife
a chopping board • a saucepan
a wooden spoon • a mixing bowl

---

1 small jar mayonnaise
4 large eggs

Tomato Dip

You will need:
a serving bowl

---

6 tablespoons tomato ketchup
225g (8oz) cream cheese

Put the cream cheese in the bowl, add the ketchup and stir until soft and smooth

Sandwich Fillings

You can fill sandwiches with anything you like, but here are some ideas for delicious mixtures:

egg mayonnaise • tuna fish and mayonnaise
grated cheese and tomato chutney • ham and cheese
grilled bacon, lettuce and tomato • mashed banana and honey
chicken, mayonnaise and celery • prawns, mayonnaise and lettuce

1. When you make party sandwiches it's easier if you use ready sliced bread.

2. Make some sandwiches with brown and some with white bread.

3. Make sure your butter is soft enough to spread easily, or use a margarine spread. Do not overfill your sandwiches.

4. Cut the crusts off.

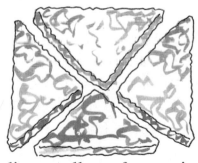

5. Cut diagonally to form triangle-shaped sandwiches.

6. Decorate with parsley or cress.

Ice Cream Sundaes

You can make ice cream sundaes with different kinds of ice cream, fruit, cream and your favourite sauces. Try some of these ideas.

Fill individual glass dishes with layers of ice cream, fresh raspberries, sliced bananas or tinned peaches. Decorate with whipped cream and your favourite sauce.

Chocolate Sauce

You will need:

a saucepan • a wooden spoon
a medium-sized bowl that will fit
over the saucepan

125g (4oz) dark chocolate
45ml (3 tablespoons) water

Toffee Sauce

You will need:

a wooden spoon • a small saucepan

30g (1oz) butter or margarine
90g (3oz) brown sugar
30ml (2 tablespoons) golden syrup
60ml (4 tablespoons) cream

Put some water in the saucepan (about a quarter full) and heat gently over a low heat. Put the 3 tablespoons of water with the chocolate in the bowl and heat over the saucepan of simmering water. As the chocolate melts you can stir it into a smooth sauce. Pour this over the ice cream and fruit.

Put the butter, sugar and syrup into the saucepan and heat gently on a low heat until they melt. Add the cream and stir until the sauce is smooth. Serve hot or cold.

Flapjacks

You will need:
a shallow, oblong baking tin • 18 x 28cm (7 x 11 inches)
a large saucepan • a wooden spoon • a tablespoon • a knife

250g (8oz) porridge oats • 125g (4oz) butter
60g (2oz) demerara sugar • 45ml (3 tablespoons) golden syrup

Oven setting: 180°C/350°F - Gas mark 4

Serves up to ten

1. Preheat the oven, and grease the baking tin. Put the sugar, syrup and butter in the saucepan and stir gently over a low heat, using the wooden spoon.

2. Take the pan off the heat, and carefully stir in the oats. Mix well together.

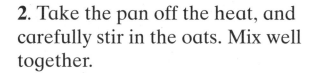

3. Spoon the mixture into the baking tin and press down well. Bake for 20 minutes until golden brown. Use oven gloves to take the baking tin out of the oven.

4. Leave the tin to cool for 5 minutes, then cut the flapjacks into fingers. When cool enough to hold, take them out of the baking tin and store in a sealed container.

These are my favourite cakes.

33

Chocolate Truffles

You will need:

a wooden spoon • a mixing bowl • a cereal bowl
a plastic container for storage • a large plate

125g (4oz) soft butter • 2 tablespoons icing sugar
6 tablespoons drinking chocolate powder
2 tablespoons cocoa powder

1. Put the butter, icing sugar and drinking chocolate into the mixing bowl, and stir well with the wooden spoon. Make it into a large ball.

2. Break off small pieces and roll them very gently between the palms of your hands to make little, round balls.

3. As you make each truffle put it on to the large plate. Keep going until you have finished up all of the mixture.

4. Put the cocoa powder into the cereal bowl and spread it out. Take a truffle and put it in the centre of the cocoa powder. Very gently move the bowl round and round, so the little ball rolls around in the cocoa and is covered all over with the powder.

5. Do this with all the truffles until they are all dusted with cocoa powder. Now put them in a plastic container to store in the fridge. Put them in paper holders to serve.

Cooking Words

bake - to cook food in the oven.

boil - to cook in boiling water.

chop - to cut food into small pieces on a chopping board.

drain - to separate liquids from solid ingredients, by putting them through a colander or sieve.

fold in - to mix an ingredient gently and slowly into a creamed mixture.

fry - to cook in hot fat or oil.

grate - to shred food, such as cheese, chocolate and bread, by rubbing it down a grater. Keep fingertips and knuckles away from the grater blades!

grease - to rub the inside of an ovenproof dish or baking tin with butter or margarine to stop food from sticking to it.

grill - to cook food under the grill.

knead - to work a dough with your hands until smooth and stretchy. This spreads the yeast throughout the bread dough.

mash - to press a fruit or vegetable with a fork or masher, until it is soft.

pinch of salt - a tiny amount of salt that you can pick up between finger and thumb.

preheat the oven - to turn the oven on some time before you want to use it for baking.

season - to add salt, pepper or other spices to food to give it more flavour.

simmer - to cook a liquid over a low heat so that it is bubbling, but not boiling.

slice - to cut food into thin rounds using a sharp knife. Always cut downwards keeping fingers well away from the blade.

whisk - to beat something hard with a whisk so that air flows in to the mixture and makes it light.